ANIMAL OPPOSITES
UP AND DOWN

1

by Cecilia Minden

Cherry Lake Publishing • Ann Arbor, Michigan

Published in the United States of America
by Cherry Lake Publishing
Ann Arbor, Michigan
www.cherrylakepublishing.com

Reading Adviser: Marla Conn, ReadAbility, Inc.

Photo Credits: © Serge Vero/Shutterstock Images, cover, 14, 16; © BMJ/Shutterstock Images, 4; © Sarah Lew/Shutterstock Images, 6; © Schubbel/Shutterstock Images, 8; © Ruslana Iurchenko/Shutterstock Images, 10; © michael sheehan/Shutterstock Images, 12, 20; © George P Gross/Shutterstock Images, 18; © Lynn Whitt/Shutterstock Images, 20; © odd-add/Shutterstock Images, 20; © Ivonne Wierink/Shutterstock Images, 20;

Library of Congress Cataloging-in-Publication Data
Up and down / by Cecilia Minden.
     pages cm.—(Animal opposites)
  Audience: K to grade 3.
  ISBN 978-1-63470-468-7 (hardcover)—ISBN 978-1-63470-588-2 (pbk.)—ISBN 978-1-63470-528-8 (pdf)—ISBN 978-1-63470-648-3 (ebook)
  1. Animals—Juvenile literature. 2. Concepts—Juvenile literature. 3. Vocabulary. I. Title.
  QL49.M677 2016
  590—dc23
                                        2015025717

Cherry Lake Publishing would like to acknowledge the work of the Partnership for 21st Century Skills. Please visit *www.p21.org* for more information.

Printed in the United States of America
Corporate Graphics

TABLE OF CONTENTS

Pets

Pets live with us. The cat **naps** up on the bed.

What Do You See?

What pattern is on the bed?

The dog is lying down on its bed.

Farm Animals

Goats live on the farm. They climb up on pieces of wood.

What Do You See?

What colors are the pig?

The pig is down in the dirt.
It likes to get muddy.

What Do You See?

What are the giraffes doing?

Zoo Animals

Giraffes live by tall trees.
They eat plants up at the top.

The lion is lying down in the grass. It likes to rest in the sun.

Water Animals

Dolphins live in the water. They swim up to the top.

Sometimes the dolphins swim down to the **bottom**.

Which animals are up?

Which animals are down?

Find Out More

BOOK

Horáček, Petr. *Animal Opposites*. Somerville, MA: Candlewick Press, 2013.

WEB SITE

The Activity Idea Place—Opposites
www.123child.com/lessonplans/other/opposites.php
Play some games to learn even more opposites.

Glossary

bottom (BAH-tuhm) the lowest or deepest part of something

dolphins (DAHL-fins) smart water animals with long snouts

giraffes (juh-RAFS) large African mammals with long necks and legs and dark brown patches on their coats

naps (NAPS) sleeps for a short time, especially during the day

Home and School Connection

Use this list of words from the book to help your child become a better reader. Word games and writing activities can help beginning readers reinforce literacy skills.

bed	goats	sun
bottom	grass	swim
by	likes	tall
cat	lion	the
climb	live	they
colors	lying	to
dirt	muddy	top
dog	naps	trees
doing	pattern	up
dolphins	pets	water
down	pieces	what
eat	pig	which
farm	plants	with
get	rest	wood
giraffes	sometimes	zoo

Index

About the Author

Cecilia Minden, PhD, is a former classroom teacher and university professor. She now enjoys working as an educational consultant and writer for school and library publications. She has written more than 150 books for children. Cecilia lives in and out, up and down, and fast and slow in McKinney, Texas.